THE WEAPONS ENCYCLOPÆDIA
TANK AIRCRAFT AFV SHIP ARTILLERY VEHICLES SECRET WEAPON

TWE-026 ENG

TANKETTE TK/TKS

THE WEAPONS ENCYCLOPAEDIA

EDITORIAL STAFF
Luca Cristini, Paolo Crippa.

ACADEMIC STAFF
Enrico Acerbi, Massimiliano Afiero, Aldo Antonicelli, Ruggero Calò, Luigi Carretta, Flavio Chistè, Anna Cristini, Carlo Cucut, Salvo Fagone, Enrico Finazzer, Arturo Giusti, Björn Huber, Andrea Lombardi, Aymeric Lopez, Marco Lucchetti, Gabriele Malavoglia, Luigi Manes, Giovanni Maressi, Francesco Mattesini, Daniele Notaro, Péter Mujzer, Federico Peirani, Alberto Peruffo, Maurizio Raggi, Andrea Alberto Tallillo, Antonio Tallillo, Roberto Vela, Massimo Zorza.

PUBLISHED BY
Luca Cristini Editore (Soldiershop), via Orio, 35/4 - 24050 Zanica (BG) ITALY.

DISTRIBUTION BY
Soldiershop - www.soldiershop.com, Amazon, Ingram Spark, Berliner Zinnfigurem (D), LaFeltrinelli, Mondadori, Libera Editorial (Spain), Google book (eBook), Kobo, (eBoook), Apple Book (eBook).

PUBLISHING'S NOTES
None of unpublished images or text of our book may be reproduced in any format without the expressed written permission of Luca Cristini Editore (already Soldiershop.com) when not indicate as marked with license creative commons 3.0 or 4.0. Luca Cristini Editore has made every reasonable effort to locate, contact and acknowledge rights holders and to correctly apply terms and conditions to Content. Every effort has been made to trace the copyright of all the photographs. If there are unintentional omissions, please contact the publisher in writing at: info@soldiershop.com, who will correct all subsequent editions.

LICENSES COMMONS
This book may utilize part of material marked with license creative commons 3.0 or 4.0 (CC BY 4.0), (CC BY-ND 4.0), (CC BY-SA 4.0) or (CC0 1.0). We give appropriate attribution credit and indicate if change were made in the acknowledgments field. Our WTW books series utilize only fonts licensed under the SIL Open Font License or other free use license.

CONTRIBUTORS OF THIS VOLUME & ACKNOWLEDGEMENTS
We would like to thank the main contributors to this issue: The profiles of the floats are all by the author. The colouring of the photos is by Anna Cristini. Special thanks to national and/or private institutions such as: Army General Staff, State Archives, Bundesarchiv, Nara, Library of Congress, Wikipedia, USAF, Signal magazine, War Chronicles, War Front, IWM, Australian War Museum, etc. A P.Crippa, A.Lopez, Péter Mujzer, L.Manes, C.Cucut, Tallillo archives. Model Victoria (www.modelvictoria.it) etc. for providing images or other items from their archives.

For a complete list of Soldiershop titles, or for every information please contact us on our website: www.soldiershop.com or www.cristinieditore.com. E-mail: info@soldiershop.com. Keep up to date on Facebook https://www.facebook.com/soldiershop.publishing

Title: **TANKETTE TK/TKS** Code.: **TWE-026 EN**
Series by L. S. Cristini
ISBN code: 979-12-5589-1291 First edition June 2024
THE WEAPONS ENCYCLOPAEDIA (SOLDIERSHOP) is a trademark of Luca Cristini Editore

THE WEAPONS ENCYCLOPÆDIA
TANK AIRCRAFT AFV SHIP ARTILLERY VEHICLES SECRET WEAPON

TANKETTE TK/TKS
POLAND'S ARMOURED COCKROACHES

LUCA STEFANO CRISTINI & PÉTER MUJZER

BOOK SERIES FOR MODELLERS & COLLECTORS

CONTENTS

Introduction... Pag. 5
  - Polish Army and the mechanisation between the wars .... Pag. 5
  - Technical features .... Pag. 7
  - Unit organisation .... Pag. 9
  - Training .... Pag. 11

Versions of the vehicle .... Pag. 13
  - Carden Loyd Mk VI .... Pag. 13
  - Polish tankette prototypes .... Pag. 16
  - Production models .... Pag. 18
  - Other experimental variants .... Pag. 19

Operational use by Polish Army .... Pag. 23
  - Polish tankettes in Hungary .... Pag. 28
  - Polish tankettes in Romania .... Pag. 36

Camouflage and markings .... Pag. 41

Data sheet .... Pag. 52

Bibliography .... Pag. 58

▲ From the Polish magazine NAC some TKS tankettes of the armoured battalion during military ceremonies and parades in the late 1930s...

INTRODUCTION

■ POLISH ARMY AND THE MECHANISATION BETWEEN THE WARS

Between the two world wars, despite the country's financial difficulties and its limited heavy industrial capacity, the Republic of Poland developed its Armed Forces on the basis of French military doctrine. The Polish military outlook was strongly influenced by the Polish-Soviet war, where in 1920, in addition to cavalry, armoured trains and armoured cars played an important role in mobile operations over the large operational area. At the outbreak of the Second World War, the Polish military leadership continued to attach great importance to the cavalry, with cavalry making up 10% of the land forces in 1939.
An autonomous operational application such as the German armoured force was far beyond the capabilities of the Polish Armed Forces, both doctrinally, financially and industrially. The Polish high command did not understand the strategic role and importance of the armoured warfare. In 1939, following French doctrine, it was preparing for static defence, attrition of the enemy on the Western front. The armoured units were assigned to support infantry and cavalry formations and not to concentrate the existing units into a mobile/armoured strike force.
The first armoured unit, the 1st Polish Tank Regiment, was organised in France on 15 March 1919 with 120 Renault FT light tanks. In the Polish Army, the armoured units, which had previously been part of the infantry, became independent units in September 1930, including 2-2 armoured car and armoured train battalions, a tank regiment and a central armoured/mechanised training school.

▲ A British Vickers Carden Loyd Mk VI light tank, on whose idea was based the entire creation of the Polish TKS and TK3 tankette series.

According to a German evaluation published in 1933, the principles of the Polish armoured troops had gone beyond the French model, and they no longer wanted to use tanks only to support infantry. In addition to supporting the infantry, the Polish concept envisaged the use of armoured battalions for independent raiding missions in support of cavalry, mechanised infantry and artillery. The idea was that mechanised units would advance on the roads and cavalry units in the field.

According to the 1936 Military Yearbook, in 1935 the Polish armoured troops consisted of 6 tank and armoured car battalions and 2 armoured train battalions, while the cavalry included 40 cavalry regiments. Poland made great efforts to develop an adequate military industrial base, and in 1939 the Polish Army was equipped almost exclusively with tankettes and light tanks and armoured cars of its own design, produced at the PZInż plant (Państwowe Zakłady Inżynierii - State Engineering Works). The Polish military industry first started to produce the TK tankettes, based on the Carden-Loyd tankette. Most of the Polish tanks and armoured cars were obsolete by 1939, but the 7TP tanks equipped with the 37 mm Bofors anti-tank gun and the TKS tankettes with the 20 mm Solothurn cannon were serious competitors for the German Pz. II-III and Lt.35 tanks. Before the war, a battalion of 45 Renault R-35 French light tanks was also added to the force.

The armoured troops consisted of light tank battalions, armoured reconnaissance battalions, independent tank, and reconnaissance tankette companies and armoured train battalions. The reconnaissance battalions and reconnaissance tankette companies were attached to the cavalry brigades and infantry divisions, while the tank battalions were attached directly to the general staff.

▲ A beautiful example of a Polish TKS tankette, with the typical camouflage of the early days, preserved at the Kubinka Armoury Museum.

TECHNICAL FEATURES

The first 82 TKS tankettes were equipped with a 6-cylinder Polski Fiat-122 AC engine, which delivered 42 HP at 2,600 RPM and had a displacement of 2,516 cm³. Starting from the 83rd TKS, the improved 6-cylinder Polski Fiat-122 BC engine was used, providing 46 HP at 2,600 RPM with a displacement of 2,952 cm³. The mechanical transmission had four forward gears and one reverse, and turning was achieved by braking one side of the track. Reinforced tracks increased the vehicle's durability off-road. The TKS could ford depths of 50 cm and cross trenches up to 100 cm wide.

For long-distance travel, the TKS had additional undercarriages with truck tires that could be mounted by removing the tracks and connecting the drive wheel to the axles of the carriage with belts, converting it into a road cart.

The TKS's armor provided adequate protection against small-arms for the crew. The first 82 TKS had front armor of 6-10 mm, side and rear armor of 5-8 mm, top armor of 3-6 mm, and bottom armor of 4 mm. From the 83rd TKS, the front armor increased to 8-10 mm, side and rear armor to 8 mm, top armor to 3-6 mm, and bottom armor to 5 mm.

A periscope designed by Rudolf Gundlach allowed a 360° view without the commander needing to turn his head. Despite its similarity to the TK-3, the TKS did not share many mechanical parts. The rear-mounted engine, with a 70-liter capacity, provided a range of 180 kilometers and a top speed of 40 km/h. The tracks were 170 mm wide with double central guide teeth.

The armament included a 7.92 mm Browning wz. 30 machine gun (with 2,000 rounds) on a universal mount with a telescopic sight, with elevation from -15° to +20° and a traverse of 48°. The two-man crew

▲ The very cramped interior of the TKS. The engine is clearly visible in the centre of the combat compartment, located between the driver and the gunner.

▲ The TK prototype No. 6007 in its final form with the roof hatches open, according to the TK-3 standard (in this case it could be a rebuilt TK-2). Note the horizontal firing angle of the machine guns and the two side observation hatches, present only in the first series TK-3s.

▼ The TKW was a prototype light tank based on the TK-3 chassis. The W in the name comes from the word *wieża*, meaning turret. This variant also had a second turret version. The prototype had no follow-up and the project was abandoned.

accessed the vehicle through two top hatches, with the driver on the left having a small viewing slot with a periscope, and the commander next to him using a rotating telescope for a 360° view. The roof also featured a mount for using the machine gun as an anti-aircraft weapon when the vehicle was stationary. During production, several changes were made, such as the installation of the less reliable Hotchkiss wz. 25 machine gun on production models, as the wz. 30s were prioritized for infantry use. From the 54th vehicle, the commander's periscope was mounted on the roof. After the first 83 tankettes, the vehicles were equipped with the Polski-Fiat 122B engine delivering 46 HP, without changes to speed and range. The weight increased to 2,570 kilograms, and in the last batches, armor thickness was further increased to between 8 and 10 mm, with 3 mm on the roof.

UNIT ORGANISATION

Light Tank Battalion

The Light Tank Battalions had a relatively modern regimentation:
- staff company with 1-1 signal, anti-aircraft machine gun, motorcycle and traffic control platoons;
- 3 light tank companies, 16 7TPs with a total of 49 tanks;
- 1 workshop/supply company.

Armoured Reconnaissance Battalion

- battalion staff and subordinated units;
- 1 armoured car companies with 7 wz. 34 armoured personnel carriers;
- 1 tankette companies 11 TK/TKS tankettes.

Reconnaissance Tankette Company

It was equipped with 11 TKS/TK tankette.

▲ Beautiful view of a TKS painted with the first type of camouflage, at the presentation of the vehicle to the Estonian authorities interested in the Polish vehicle in 1934.

▲ A well-made replica with the tankette armed with a 20mm heavy machine gun.

Mechanised Cavalry Brigades

The Polish Mechanised Troops included two mechanised cavalry brigades, which were rearmed from the existing cavalry units. In 1937, the Polish Ministry of Defence approved the creation of an experimental mechanised/armoured brigade. Thus, in 1937-1938, the 10th Mechanised Cavalry Brigade was formed, with the existing cavalry regiments being rearmed into mechanised regiments, retaining their original names and organisation.

The 10th Mechanised Cavalry Brigade

- 2 mechanised cavalry regiments (4 mechanised cavalry squadron, 1 machine-gun, 1 sapper, motorcycle and anti-tank gun platoon each);
- 1 reconnaissance battalion (1 tankette and mechanised rifle squadron, 1-1 signal, motorcycle, machine gun and anti-tank gun platoons);
- 1 motorised engineer battalion;
- 1 motorised anti-tank battalion (2 anti-tank gun companies);
- 1 motorised field artillery battalion;
- 1 motorised anti-aircraft gun battery;
- 1 light tank company;
- 1 tankette company;
- 1 motorised signal company;
- 1 motorised supply company;
- 1 traffic-control motorcycle platoon.

The brigade's armament consisted of 46 machine guns, four 81 mm mortars, twentyseven 37 mm Bofors anti-tank guns, four 75 mm gun field guns, four 100 mm field howitzers, four 40 mm Bofors anti-aircraft guns, 26 TK/TKS tankettes and 16 Vickers light tanks. The motor pool included 77 cars, 290 trucks, 57 artillery tractors and 260 motorcycles.

The second unit, the Warsaw mechanised brigade, was only organised in June 1939 and had not yet reached full combat readiness at the outbreak of war. The brigade's organisation was roughly the same as that of the 10th Mechanised Cavalry Brigade. Its light tank company was equipped with 16 7TP light tanks.

On 1 September 1939, the Polish armoured regiments consisted of the following units and combat vehicles; 3 light tank battalions, 11 armoured reconnaissance battalions, 19 reconnaissance tankette companies and 5 light tank companies. The armoured troops consisted of 377 TK/TKS tankettes, 98 7TP, 49 R-35, 34 Vickers and 45 Renault FT 17 light tanks, and 88 WZ. 29th and 34th armoured personnel carriers, for a total of 691 combat vehicles. The Poles also had 10 armoured trains.

■ TRAINING

The Armoured and Motor Vehicle Officer School was founded in Warsaw in 1920, where dozens of officers were trained in combat and motor vehicle engineering. In 1930 the School was dissolved and the Armoured Training Centre was established, which was transferred to the Modlin Fortress in 1934 as the Armoured and Armoured Vehicle Training Centre. An experimental tank battalion was organised in its cadre, with one company each of tankettes and armoured cars. From 1927, the School for Officers of Tanks and Armoured Vehicles was established in Warsaw. Crews were trained in the Biedrusk Armoured Training Camp for operating armoured vehicles and for combat training; initially only individual training was given. Later, training was carried out in platoons and, from the mid-1930s, in company and battalion formations.

From the mid-1930s, the development of armoured and mechanised troops demanded an increasing number of trained officers. The Armoured Tank and Armoured Vehicle Training Centre set up the Reserve Armoured Officers School and organised a 9-month course for armoured officers. The officer and reserve officer schools had a staff of 180-180 officer candidates. Between the two world wars, approximately 10,000 officers, non-commissioned officers and enlisted men were trained.

According to a report compiled by the commander of the 10th Mechanised Cavalry Brigade after its defeat in 1939, the shortcomings of the armoured brigade (actually mechanised) were; neglect of reconnaissance, shortage of armour and artillery, lack of air cover, unreliable communications, insufficient repair/technical staff, inadequate medical cover and lack of all-terrain vehicles.

Poland made great efforts to create an armoured corps, but the armoured units, which adhered to French doctrine and were equipped with obsolete home-made armour, were only used to support the infantry and cavalry.

▲ Parade of Estonian weapons. In the foreground a newly acquired Polish tankette, mid-1930s.

TK-2 TANKETTE PROTOTYPE, POLAND 1930

▲ One of the first prototypes made from the British Vickers Carden Loyd Mk VI light tank.

VERSIONS OF THE VEHICLE

■ CARDEN-LOYD MK.VI

British tank building experiments echoed throughout the world. The "six-ton Vickers" birthed a family of tanks that fought for several nations in WWII. The history of the Polish tankettes, just like of most of world's tankettes, started with two British designers: John Carden and Vivian Loyd. In 1925-1928 years, they designed several light one-man, then two-men tracked fighting vehicles. In that period, there was a popular idea of a light armoured vehicle, being a mean of transport for one or two soldiers and a machine gun. Several designers in the world developed such vehicles, nick-named "tankettes", for they were smaller, than "real" tanks. The most successful among them was Carden-Loyd Two Man Tankette Mark VI of 1928. These tankettes were produced in the USSR (T-27), France, Czechoslovakia, Japan, Italy, Poland. In the last two countries, tankettes were the majority of tracked armoured vehicles by the start of the war. The Carden-Loyd Mk.VI was armed with a water-cooled Vickers 7.7mm infantry heavy machine gun, mounted on an external pivot mount. Its drive mechanism was simple, utilizing some car parts, including a popular Ford T car engine placed between crew seats. Turns were made simply braking one track. An armoured crew compartment had no roof, though head covers were introduced soon in export models. The improved Mk.VIb was more compact, with a new hull and a closed combat compartment. In 1929, its mass production in Britain began, and Poland bought one unit for trials.

Since the Carden-Loyd Mk.VI tankette was widely advertised in the world, also for a usage as an armoured tractor, mortar carrier or a gun carrier, it met with a great commercial success, as for its period. An advantage of tankettes was their low price, so they were ideal for creating and training armoured forces. On the other hand, as the future showed, they all had little combat value, and could not be a cheaper alternative of tanks in a battlefield. Apart from the British Army, which used 348 Carden-Loyd

▲ Tankette TKS on display at the Polish Army Museum.

tankettes in different variants, mostly machine gun carriers, they were sold to at least 16 countries; in small numbers, though. Six countries bought manufacture rights, but none produced the original model in significant numbers. Instead, some countries developed improved derivatives or own tankettes, influenced by Carden-Loyd. First of all it was the USSR, where 3297 of much improved licence tankettes T-27 were produced in 1931-1934. The Italians first built 21 licence tankettes CV-29, then started mass production of an indigenous design CV-33 / CV-35, inspired by Carden-Loyd (Italy found itself in a similar situation to Poland, with armoured divisions consisting mostly of tankettes, which showed little combat value in the Spanish Civil War, then in Africa). Also Czechoslovakia developed an improved derivative *tančik* vz.33 (name meaning ‹small tank›, 70 built), and similar own prototype Skoda MU-4. Among these countries was also Poland.

■ CARDEN-LOYD IN POLAND

The Carden-Loyd Mk.VI met with an interest in Poland from the beginning. As soon as in 1929 one tankette was brought and evaluated in Poland. The first show at Rembertow ground took place on 20 June 1929. The first trials were successful and it was decided to buy 10 tankettes Mk.VI and 5 tracked trailers. They were delivered in August 1929 and given registration numbers: 1143-1152. After divisional manoeuvres in September 1929, it was evaluated, that tankettes fulfil well needs of a reconnaissance vehicle for both infantry and cavalry. Their advantages were: mobility, good obstacle crossing and small dimensions, making them difficult to spot. It was estimated, that they fit better as cavalry reconnaissance vehicles, than newly acquired wz.28 halftrack armoured cars. As a result, the Polish authorities decided to buy a licence for manufacturing Carden-Loyd Mk.VI.

▲ Front view of the self-propelled tankette.

TK-3 TANKETTE, POLAND 1936

▲ TK-3 tankette of the 6th Tank Battalion in Lwów, Poland, 3 May 1936.

Detailed evaluation revealed faults of the Carden-Loyd tankette, though. First of all, its suspension did not spring well, and riding was not comfortable, so longer ride was exhausting for a crew, especially off-road. As a result, the suspension in two tankettes was modified in the workshops of the 1st Car Unit, according to a design by Lt. Stanisław Marczewski. The main improvement was adding a semi-elliptical leaf spring between a hull and suspension bogies, and attaching bogies to this spring, instead of a suspension frame. Also return rollers were added. The new suspension improved ride comfort much, and was the most successful design used in Carden-Loyd influenced tankettes. However, instead of producing Carden-Loyd Mk.VI, the Polish authorities decided to work an own, improved model, only generally basing on Carden-Loyd's composition. Probably only two Mark VIs were manufactured in Poland, of mild iron. Carden-Loyd (CL) tankettes were next assigned to the Experimental Armoured-Motorized Group. In the following years, they were used in manoeuvres and for training. Their eventual fate is not known, probably some were broken into parts.

■ PROTOTYPES OF THE POLISH TANKETTES

The task of designing the Polish tankette was assigned to the Armoured Weapons Construction Bureau of the Army Engineer Research Institute (BK Br.Panc. WIBI) in Warsaw. Main designers were Maj. Władysław Trzeciak and Cpt. Edward Karkoz, with a cooperation of Edward Habich. The new design was worked in two variants, differing in suspension and drive gear layout. In 1930, the State Engineering Works (PZInż.) in Warsaw built two prototypes: TK-1 with sprocket wheels in the rear and TK-2 with sprocket wheels in front. They were generally modelled after Carden-Loyd in composition, but were completely new designs, more compact and differing in shape. Their suspension was similar to Carden-Loyd suspension modified by S. Marczewski. Tracks were modified and strengthened, made of manganese steel. TK-2 had Ford T engine (like Carden-Loyd), TK-1 - newer Ford A engine. Unlike to the

▲ One of the most interesting versions operated on the Polish tankette was the self-propelled TKD version.

TKS TANKETTE, POLAND (HUNGARY BY INCORPORATION), 1939

▲ TKS (20 mm) reconnaissance vehicle of the 101st Reconnaissance Company of the 10th Motorised Cavalry Brigade. Hungary, October 1939.

Carden-Loyd, both were fitted with electric starters. Both vehicles had an open crew compartment and were armed with an air-cooled 7.92 mm Hotchkiss wz.25 machine gun. As for the name of the Polish tankette, there is no single opinion about its origins. TK can stand for the last names of the designers who worked on the project, Tszeczak and Karkoza, the initials of Lieutenant Colonel Tadeusz Kossakowski, from the engineering department of the Polish Army, or just an abbreviation of the word "tankette".

The TK-1 prototype carried a registration number 6006, the TK-2 probably 6007 and another prototype TK-3 probably 6008. Also, two TK prototypes were ordered on 20 March 1930, which were licence copies of Carden-Loyd built of mild iron and completed on 17 May 1930.

In August-September 1930 both TK prototypes took part in divisional manoeuvres, along with Carden-Loyd tankettes. After trials, the construction bureau was ordered to improve the design further. It was fitted with a fully closed combat compartment and given a military designation: "fast tank TK wz.31". Both prototypes were sent to the factory to rebuild them with closed compartments. Also, the third improved prototype designated TK-3 was ordered, with a closed compartment and a modified suspension with sprocket wheels in front. Improved prototypes and the TK-3 were completed in March 1931. Probably the TK-2 was completely rebuilt to TK-3 standard, with improved suspension. After trials, prototypes TK-2 and TK-3 were kept in PZInż factory as a production pattern.

■ PRODUCTION MODELS

TK-3 (TK) TANKETTE

On 14 July 1931, the Chief of the General Staff accepted the TK-3 prototype, and ordered the first batch of 100 tanks, as a light reconnaissance tank TK-3 (also known simply as the TK). The first information series of 15 tanks (numbers 1154-1168) was built of mild iron plates instead of armour plates. They were completed in August 1931 and just in September sent to divisional manoeuvres. These so-called "iron" tanks were not fit to combat and were later used for training and converting to other designs. The remaining 85 tankettes were made of armoured plates and completed by May 1932. The second batch of 100 tankettes were built by August 1932 - they both were numbered 1169-1353. The last series of 100 tankettes had numbers 1362-1461. A total of 300 TK-3 tankettes, including 15 "iron" ones, were built. This number probably includes also TKF tankettes.

TKF TANKETTE

Since the TK-3 was powered with an imported engine Ford A, it was decided to replace it with Polski FIAT-122BC engine, licence-built in Poland. It was first experimentally fitted in the TK-3 nr. 1221 in late 1931 or 1932. In 1933, there was manufactured a small series of tankettes with FIAT engines, designated TKF («F» for FIAT), but their number is not exactly known - 18 to 22. The information about these vehicles is not clear. Apparently, they were included in the last ordered TK-3 series. The production of TKF was discontinued, because an improved model TKS was developed. Probably from 1935 they were modernized using TKS suspension parts and wider tracks, so they had better traction and stronger and more reliable suspension. The most significant differences were: an idler wheel suspension and a front frame connector shape. Apart from it, the TKF did not differ externally from the TK-3. A modification of all TK-3 to TKF standard was considered, but abandoned due to costs.

TKS TANKETTE

In 1933 there started works upon an improved tankette model. The main designer became Edward Habich (after Maj. Trzeciak's death). The new model was generally based upon TK-3 design, but only few parts remained interchangeable. First of all, a hull shape was changed and armour made a bit thicker to increase protection against bullets, and to give a driver a better view. The Ford A engine was replaced with Polski FIAT-122, with a new drive gear. The suspension was strengthened and tracks made 3 cm wider for better traction. The machine gun was mounted in an universal ball mounting with telescopic sights. In a course of production, a significant improvement was a modern reversible periscope for a commander, that enabled all around observation. It was the Polish invention of Rudolf Gundla, next sold to Vickers-Armstrong company and popularized in the world as Tank Periscope Mk.IV. The driver was given a simple periscope in his vision slot. The prototype TKS was converted of one of "iron" TK-3s, nr. 1160, and completed on 1 April 1933. The tank was first designated STK ('special TK'), finally TKS, in documents also written as TKS. It was also officially designated as the "fast tank wz.33", but designations "wz. .." are never used for serial TK and TKS in any sources, and the Army recognized them just as TK-3 and TKS.

After successful prototype trials, the PZInż manufactured 20 pre-series tankettes TKS, made of mild iron, in August 1933 (nos. 1492-1511). After minor improvements, the tank was accepted for a serial production on 22 February 1934. The prototype was initially armed with a water-cooled wz.30 machine gun, but in serial tanks it was replaced with the standard air-cooled wz.25 machine gun, despite better reliability of the wz.30. Starting from the 54th serial tank, the Gundlach periscope was mounted on the roof, what demanded lowering a muffler in order to obtain a clear field of view rearwards. The first series of 83 tanks was completed by June 1934. From the 83rd tank, the 42HP engine Polski FIAT-122AC was changed to the 46HP Polski FIAT-122BC. In the last series, an armour thickness slightly increased. Totally, 282 TKS tankettes were produced until April 1937, including 20 «iron» ones (serial numbers: 1-262, registration numbers: 1492-1594, 1597-1682, 1702-1764, 1799-1814 and some from among 8890-8910). Apparently 10 additional tankettes were manufactured of funds of the PZInż workers and given to the Army on 15 May 1938.

TANKETTES WITH 20 MM GUN

There were several ideas to re-arm the tankettes with more powerful weapons. Since it was obvious, that tankettes armed with machine guns cannot fight against any armoured vehicles, it was proposed to arm some of them with a cannon. A proposal was made in 1931 to use the 13.2 mm Hotchkiss heavy machinegun. Variants with 37 and even 45 mm guns were explored. In 1935-36, the heavy 20 mm Solothurn S-18-100 anti-tank rifle (used as the primary armament on the Hungarian Toldi tank) was tested on a TKS tankette. The trials showed that it could be useful to install a weapon of this caliber, but idea was rejected as the rifle could only fire single shots. After testing out several models of Oerlikon, Solothurn, and Madsen autocannons, a decision was made in August of 1939 to re-arm 80 TKS and 70 TK-3 tankettes with the recently designed 20 mm wz.38 model A guns.

Only 50 guns were made before the war, and even fewer were actually installed on tankettes: between 20 and 24. There were also plans to rearm TK tankettes with cannons, what demanded adding a front superstructure, making it similar to the TKS. It was planned to rearm 16 tankettes TK by 25 August 1939, but there is no evidence, that they were completed before the outbreak of the war.

Combining their small size, good mobility, and improved armament, these TKS and TK-3 tankettes were among the most useful of the Polish tank fleet.

EXPERIMENTAL VARIANTS AND FURTHER DEVELOPMENT

Several vehicles were developed from the TK and TKS. Apart from the C2P tractor, they did not enter production:

Any story of Polish tankettes should mention experimental vehicles on their chassis. In late 1932 or early 1933, an experimental TKW (W for wieża, turret) turreted version of the tankette was built. Both air- and water-cooled machineguns were tried out. Experiments with this tankette showed that it was extremely cramped, had terrible air flow, and bad visibility. The center of gravity was too high and the right side was overloaded, which could lead to it flipping over. The driver's armoured cabin restricted to turret's rotation to a 306-degree arc.

The TKD self-propelled gun was built on the TK-3 chassis in 1932, armed with a 47 mm short barreled Vickers QF gun. The SPGs were meant for anti-tank and artillery support of cavalry units. Exercises in the summer of 1933 showed that there were no problems with the suspension, but the weak gun was inadequate for the needs of the Polish Army. One experimental TKS-D vehicle was armed with a 37 mm Bofors gun. The concept was unique: the tankette served as a tractor for an anti-tank gun, which could be removed from its mount and installed in the tankette if necessary, turning the tractor into a miniature tank destroyer.

Another interesting design was the Polish take on the convertible drive concept which was popular in the 1930s. A special wheeled chassis was designed for tankettes on the Ursus A truck chassis. After driving up a ramp, the drive sprockets connected to the rear axle with chains and the controls were connected to the front wheels. The tankettes took on the shape of heavy armoured cars, although the lack of turret meant that this solution was of questionable utility in combat.

- TKW - TK tankette with a rotating turret (1 prototype);
- TKS-B - TKS tankette with an improved chassis and a transmission with side clutches (1 prototype);
- TKD - self-propelled 47mm wz.25 Pocisk infantry gun (4 experimental vehicles);
- TKS-D tank destroyer - self-propelled 37mm wz.36 Bofors anti-tank gun (2 prototypes);
- C2P - light artillery tractor (serial production).

There was also some special equipment developed for tankettes and used in tankette units: a tracked universal trailer, a radio trailer, a wheeled chassis for transporting by own power («autotransport») and a rail chassis for the usage in armoured trains.

▲ Polish tank drivers intent on repairing something in the area of the wheel tracks of their vehicle.

TK-3 TANKETTE, POLAND 1939

▲ TK-3 reconnaissance tank of the 81st Armoured Battalion of the Pomeranian Cavalry Brigade, Poland, September 1939.

▲ Late production TKS in the new camouflage (late variant), at the Ursus factory workers' celebration in 1938.

▼ Various Polish TK3 tankettes engaged in military tests and field exercises in 1938.

OPERATIONAL USE

The TK-3, TKF, and TKS tankettes were the backbone of the Polish armoured force before WWII. 600 units formed a mighty Army on paper. In reality, they could not serve as a proper replacement for "real" tanks. However, advantages such as small size and good mobility let them perform reconnaissance or fight from ambushes. In the absence of other armour, they could perform the role of an infantry support tank, their presence alone sometimes boosting the morale of Polish infantry and negatively impacting the Germans, who were not expecting to encounter Polish armour.

One of the first large battles of WWII began on September 9th, 1939; the Battle of the Bzura. Polish Poznan and Pomorze Armies, retreating to the east from the Poznan salient, ended up in the rear of the German Army Group South, which was aiming towards Warsaw. Moving at night, the Poles secretly reached the Bzura river and delivered a powerful blow against the left flank of the German 8th Army. The south-east offensive liberated many cities and forced the Germans to revise their plans in central Poland, moving additional tank and airplane units towards Bzura. The situation was so critical for the Germans that on September 17th, the Luftwaffe cancelled all sorties except those in the Bzura region. Nevertheless, the Poznan and Pomorze Armies were unable to change the overall course of events; the Germans were at Lvov on September 12th and completed the encirclement of Warsaw on September 14th.

Among other units, the Great Poland Cavalry Brigade was a part of the Poznan Army, which in turn contained the 71st Armoured Battalion. Out of the three companies of this unit, formed just before the war (August 24th-27th), only one was equipped with vehicles which would be referred to as tanks. These were 13 machinegun-armed TKS (and possibly TK-3) tankettes, four of which were rearmed to 20 mm wz. 38 model A autocannons, classified as "super-heavy machineguns" by the Poles. One of these "heavily" armed tankettes ended up under the command of a platoon commander Sergeant Roman Edmund

▲ Polish tankettes took part in the Polish occupation of Czechoslovakia 1938. When the Germans triggered the Sudetenland crisis, Czechoslovakia's neighbouring nations also took advantage of it, among them the Poles.

Orlik, a student of the Warsaw Polytechnical University, drafted on August 26th. The second member of the crew was the driver, Bronisław Zakrzewski.

During the Battle of the Bzura, the Great Poland Cavalry Brigade fought fiercely against the 4th Tank Division of the XVI Motorized Corps, 10th Army. On September 14th, the brigade attacked at Brochów. In this battle, Orlik destroyed 3 tanks from the 36th Tank Regiment. Likely these were PzI and PzII tanks, as they made up the majority of the tanks in the 4th division.

On September 18th, the Great Poland Cavalry Brigade, now a part of the Operational Cavalry Group, formed to clear the path to Warsaw for the rest of the elements of the Poznan Army who were being encircled by Germans, was fighting near the Kampinoski Park, west of the capital. Orlik's platoon (in Polish sources, a half-platoon, półpluton), his tankette and two more armed with machineguns were sent out to scout. Hearing the noise of tank engines ahead, the sergeant ordered the machinegun tankettes to hide and put his own tankette in an ambush position.

A column of three tanks and several cars from the 1st German Light Division was driving along the road. Opening fire suddenly, Orlik knocked out the front tank with a shot to the side, forcing the rest of the vehicles to drive into the forest to go around. Changing positions, Orlik destroyed the other two tanks. The rest of the column fled, and his platoon left the battle with no losses.

Several sources claim that the tanks he destroyed were Czech PzKpfw 35(t) tanks, since those were the most common in the 1st Light Division, but one of the tanks was likely a PzIV. The division had several tanks of this time, and lost 9 of them between September 1st and September 25th. Wiktor IV Albrecht von Ratibor was among the heavily wounded in this battle, and later died. Several sources state that he commanded a PzIV crew, and there is even a photograph of his destroyed tank.

On September 19th, Orlik took part in the Battle for Sieraków, where a few dozen tanks of the German 11th Tank Regiment and 65th Tank Battalion attacked the Polish 7th Mounted Rifle Regiment and 9th

▲ The image of defeat. A German soldier pauses to observe the damage inflicted on this tankette equipped with a 20 mm machine gun. Note the track strip sticking out of the roof of the vehicle.

TKS 20 mm TANKETTE, POLAND 1939

▲ TKS (20 mm) reconnaissance tank of the Warsaw Motorised Brigade, Poland, September 1939.

▲ Row of Polish tankettes captured (and later re-used) by the Germans during the Blitzkrieg.
▼ Rear view of a TDK half camouflaged with foliage during operations in 1939.

TK-3 TANKETTE, POLAND 1939

▲ TK-3 with first type of camouflage. Poland 1939.

Lancer Regiment. More than 20 German tanks were destroyed by the Polish tankers and towed guns from the 7th towed artillery squadron, 7 of which were claimed by Orlik. He also captured two German tankers prisoner. After that, Orlik managed to drive his tankette to Warsaw, take part in its defense, and then join the Polish resistance after its fall. He survived the war and worked as an architect.

Taking his vehicle into account, his achievements (13 knocked out or destroyed tanks in less than a week) are pretty amazing. The small, lightly armoured, and lightly armed TKS tankette looks nothing like a menacing tank destroyer. Nevertheless, practice showed that it can be a deadly weapon in the right hands. Seeing as how Orlik became a tanker several days before the war, mastering it wasn't hard. A captured German tank officer as saying "It's hard to hit a small cockroach with a gun".

POLISH TANKETTES IN HUNGARY

Due to the German and later the Soviet onslaught Polish refugees and troops started to take refuge in Hungary from mid-September.

The commander of the 10th Motorised Cavalry Brigade, Colonel Maczek was ordered to withdraw from Stanislawów to Hungarian territory. The 10th Cavalry Brigade passed the border on 19 September 1939 at Tatár (Tatarow) Pass, the troops gathered on Hungarian soil at Rahó (Racho) and Bustyánháza (Busti Haza). The Motorised Cavalry Brigade bivouac at Rahó (Racho) on 20 September. The Brigade took part in heavy fighting against the Germans. Lost 10% of the men and 30% of the officers, but could save most of their equipment. They crossed the border with 651 motor vehicles, according to other sources the numbers were 874. The 101st Reconnaissance Tank Company brought 12-15 TK/TKS tankettes to Hungary.

The status of the Polish military personnel was clear from the very beginning based on the international law; they were not prisoners of war, as Hungary and Poland were not at war. They were interned military

▲ After the sudden collapse following the German invasion, some Polish troops retreated to Hungary in 1939 with their vehicles, which would later be confiscated by the Hungarian Army.

TK-3 TANKETTE, POLAND 1939

▲ TK-3 tank of an unidentified unit. Poland 1939.

TANKETTE TK/TKS

▲▼ After the heavy defeat, many vehicles ended up in the hands of the victors: tankettes and several cannons can be seen above. The photo below, which is more emblematic, simply explains the gap between German and Polish armament, with the small tankette with a Panzer II and IV.

TK-3 SCOUT TANKETTE, POLAND 1939

▲ The Polish Army had around 300 TK-3s in September 1939. By that time, the TK-3s were already quite outdated. They were nevertheless used in the front line.

personnel, a different category, much lenient rules were applicable than being a POW (prison of war). However, the equipment was a different story. The records are fragmented due to the lost Hungarian files, destroyed at the end of the WW2. But from the very beginning, it was clear that the Hungarian Army wanted to take over and use first of all the Polish military vehicles. The Chief of Staff gave guidelines regarding the collection, evaluation, repair, and distribution of Polish-origin vehicles. According to a report from January 1940, the Hungarian Army had 16 TK/TKS tankettes and 3 Renault R-35 medium (according to the Hungarian records) tanks from the ex-Polish source. One armoured car also mentioned in the records, but no further information available, probably it was a WW1 vintage and written of on arrival.

The armoured vehicles, due to their small numbers, were used as training vehicles. The Polish and Czech vehicles were distributed among the reconnaissance and armoured cavalry battalions. According to the instruction of the Chief of Staff of the Army, the captured Czech and interned Polish tanks were used for basic armoured training at the battalions to save the Toldi light tanks, Ansaldo tankettes and Csaba armoured cars from the inexperienced crew.

In late 1939, the Polish TK/TKS tankets first were grouped at the reconnaissance and armoured cavalry battalions, later in 1940, were distributed among the bicycle battalions too. Each bicycle battalion had one tankette platoon with six 35M FIAT Ansaldo tankettes.

Based on a report from the 1st Reconnaissance Battalion, dated 15 April 1940, altogether 13 repairable and 5 written off Polish tankettes arrived to the maintenance platoon of the Battalion. The written off vehicles were used to provide spare parts for the repairable ones. The 1st Reconnaissance Battalion also requested nine new batteries for the tankettes, as only four arrived earlier. According to another letter of the 1st Motorised Brigade, they got 14 TK/TKS tankettes to put them into service and not 16, which number mentioned in another report. The brigade reported that they had 14 tankettes, one of them unserviceable and proposed to distribute the armoured vehicles as follows: 1st Reconnaissance battalion four, 2nd Reconnaissance, 1st and 2nd Armoured Cavalry Battalions three-three ex-Polish tankettes, the one unserviceable one went to the Military Automobile Depot on 07 May 1940.

▲ A tankette captured and tested by Wehrmacht officers.

▲ TKS Polish Tankette front and back view.

▲ Other tankettes ended up in German hands readapted for use and recoloured in feld grau with the addition of German white crosses. September 1939, in Ruda Pabianicka (today a district of Łódź).

▼ Parade of TKS tankettes of the Panzer East light company in Warsaw after the Polish conflict.

TK-3 TANKETTE, POLAND 1939

▲ TK-3 reconnaissance tank of the 51st Armoured Battalion, Poland, 1939.

The TK/TKS tankettes with number plates: wz-02552, wz-01089, wz-02754, 0z-03586 original served at the 1st Reconnaissance Battalion. The TK/TKS tankettes of wz-02246, wz-03368, and wz-13362 were at the 2nd Reconnaissance Battalion. The 1st Armoured Cavalry Battalion had the TK/TKS tankettes of wz-02738, wz-03292 and wz-04107. The 2nd Armoured Cavalry Battalion had the tankettes wz-03893, wz-01768, wz- 03923. The TK/TKS, wz-02470 was at the Hungarian Army Automobile Depot at Mátyásföld for evaluation.

In 1941 the TK/TKS tankettes wz-02552 served at the 1st Reconnaissance Battalion, the wz-01089 was at 10th Bicycle Battalion, the wz-02754 was at the 12th Bicycle and the wz-03586 served at the 13th Bicycle Battalion.

The TK/TKS tankette, wz-02246 served at the 2nd Reconnaissance, the wz-03368 was at the 14th Bicycle, the wz-13362 served at 15th Bicycle battalions. The wz-02738 was at the 1st Armoured Cavalry battalion, the wz-03292 posted to the 2nd Armoured Cavalry, the wz-04107 was sent to the 16th Bicycle Battalions. The tankettes wz-03893, wz-01768 and wz-03923 remained with the 2nd Armoured Cavalry, as well as the wz-02470 at the Automobile Depot at Mátyásföld.

One of the TK tankettes, belonged to the 1st Cavalry Tank Battalion at Zenta from 1942. It was captured by the Yugoslavian partisans when the Hungarians withdrew from Zenta and left behind the unserviceable tankette. Currently, this TK tankette is exhibited in Belgrade.

POLISH TANKETTES IN ROMANIA

Before the war Romania and Poland were in a military alliance against the predicted offensive of the Soviet Union. In case of an attack of any allied nation, the other had to provide military support to the other nation against the onslaught of the Red Forces. However, after 17 September it was clear for the Polish political and military leadership, that the Romanian military support could not turn the Red tide and save Poland. Romania was officially released from the obligation of the Polish-Romanian military

▲ Rare and famous original colour photo of a Polish TK-3 taken by Hugo Jaeger. The tankette still bears the original insignia with the famous sword arm. Small photo: tankette in use by Lutfwaffe personnel.

alliance. In return the Romanian authorities helped the withdrawing Polish forces into the so called "Romanian bridgehead". The withdrawing Polish troops crossed the border with their weapons and equipment, the weapons were confiscated and used by the Romanian Armed Forces. According to the information beside one R-35 tank battalion Polish TK/TKS tankettes also reached Romania, probably used for training.

▲ German east front column 1941. In the foreground the self-propelled TKD. In the small photos: on the left feld grau TKF tankette, essentially a TK-3 with a new engine. On the right a German soldier posing.

▲ Column of German TKS on parade.

▼ The Polish TK-3 tankette was used as the basis of the TKD. In the process, as can be seen in the image below, the overall frame design remained largely unchanged.

TKS TANKETTE, POLAND 1939

TANKETTE TK/TKS

▲ View of the Polish TKS tankette from above

CAMOUFLAGE AND MARKINGS

■ EARLY CAMOUFLAGE

Between 1932 and 1936, the Polish armoured vehicles used an early camouflage scheme, commonly called: "the Japanese camouflage" in Poland. Its normative source has not been found in archives so far, therefore there are some doubts concerning the colours used. According to the newest research, basing on examination of museal items, it consisted of big irregular patches of yellowish sand, olive green and light blue-gray, separated with thin black stripes; blue-gray being the lightest shade. Traditional publications commonly quoted dark brown colour instead of blue-gray, and considered sand the lightest shade. There was a standard pattern of patches initially, but many tanks featured different patterns or had some colours inverted. The interior was blue-gray, inner surfaces of hatches were camouflaged.
Before an introduction of the "Japanese" camouflage, five "iron" TK-3 of the first series were experimentally painted in black and white patches, five in blue-gray overall and five in yellow and green patches.

■ LATE CAMOUFLAGE

From 1936 on there was a new standard three-colour camouflage scheme introduced for all the Polish military vehicles. It consisted of irregular patches of greyish sand and dark brown (sepia) airbrushed over a base color of olive-green. The patches had soft transitions, their shapes were mainly horizontal, often close to rectangular or rhomboid. There was not any standard pattern of patches, although the patterns used were similar (the instruction gave example views of front and right side of the TKS only). Often the patches created a kind of a chessboard, especially on late series vehicles. Transitions between colours are often inconspicuous on black and white photos. An interior was painted sand, including hatches.
Almost all tankettes were repainted in the new camouflage in the late 1930s, only some of tankettes used as armoured draisines of armoured trains and possibly some training vehicles remained in the old camouflage in September 1939.

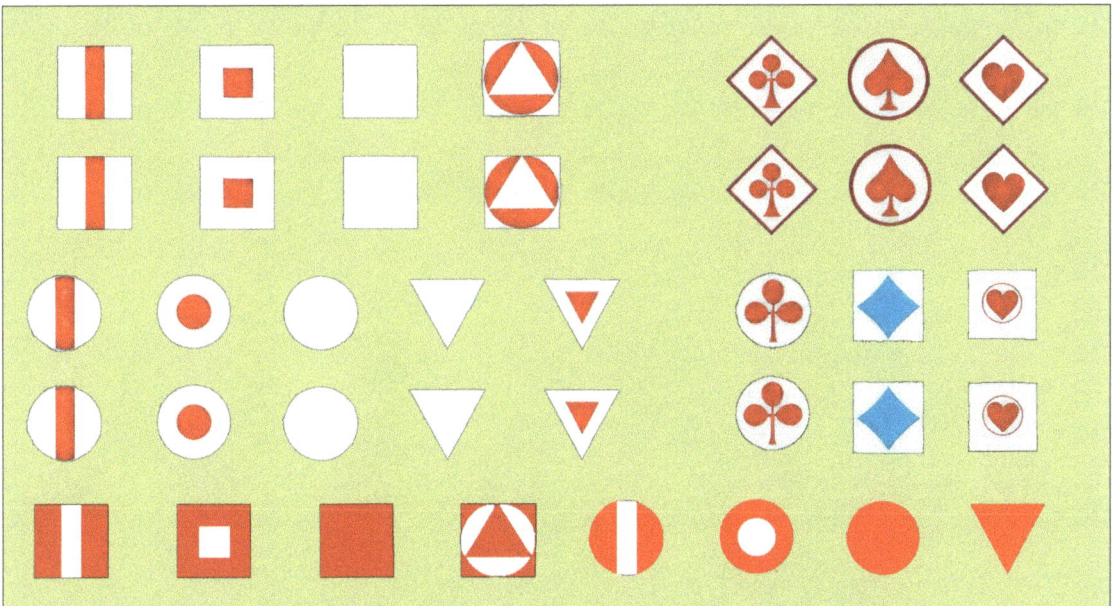

▲ Various distinguishing marks of Polish chariots. Like the French, the Poles adopted the card suits.

MARKINGS

From the early 1930s until 1939, the Polish armoured vehicles carried no nationality signs in any form. Before the war, there were used tactical signs of metal sheet attached for training purpose - discs (the 1st platoon), triangles (the 2nd) or squares (the 3rd). The signs were white with a vertical red stripe for a platoon commander, or with a small red disc, triangle or square inside for the 2nd in command. Squadron commanders had a sign of a triangle in a circle in a square. Their colors could also be inverted.

In September 1939, the tankettes generally carried no insignia at all. Usage of any insignia was forbiden in case of war by the regulation from 1938, nonetheless there are several photos known of tankettes captured in September 1939, still carrying tactical signs. The photos from 1939 also show a few cases of unofficial unit and possibly individual insignia painted on tankettes (Pomerania's Griffon for TK-3s of the 81st Armoured Unit, arrows for TK-3 of an unknown unit, rocking horse - possibly on a tank of the 10th Cavalry Brigade, and one photo of a sword-armed hand on TK-3). Four-digit registration numbers were painted on front plates only until 1936, then registration plates with new numbers were carried inside.

▲ During tankette tests in Estonia, the vehicles appeared with the first type of camouflage.

OTHER USERS

- **Croatia**: the independent State of Croatia, created by the Germans after the dismemberment of Yugoslavia in April 1941, acquired several TKF and TKS armored vehicles from Germany or Hungary between late 1941 and early 1942. These vehicles, used by both the Army and the Ustashe, were known as "Ursus tanks".

- **Estonia**: in November 1934, Poland sold six TKS tankettes to Estonia. These vehicles were the only modern armored vehicles available to the Baltic country. Subsequently, they entered the ranks of the Red Army when the USSR annexed Estonia in the summer of 1940.

- **Germany**: after the military campaign in Poland, the Third Reich captured most of the TK-3 and TKS tankettes, many of which were damaged or without fuel. These vehicles were initially sporadically reused, but between 1940 and 1941, they were sent to Łódź for repairs. It is estimated that between 50 and 100 units were maintained, repainted in the standard color for armored vehicles (Panzergrau), and marked with black and white crosses as identification symbols. The more numerous TKS received the new designation of Pzkpfw TKS (p) ("p" for polnische, meaning Polish in German) and were used as artillery tractors and for public order and anti-partisan tasks. Some entered the Luftwaffe for airfield defense. The TK-3 were renamed Pzkpfw TK-3 (p) and assigned the same tasks as the TKS. The Polish tanks were rearmed with MG 15 or MG 34 7.92 mm machine guns, and in at least one case, the ball joint was replaced with a plate featuring a sight and a gun port. Two headlights were also added above the side fenders. Both models operated throughout the conflict and were found in France, Norway, and Finland. In June 1940, the Germans created a security unit equipped solely with 7TP, TKS, and TK-3 tanks, the Leichte Panzerkompanie Warschau (Warsaw Light Tank Company), which on September 3rd changed its name to Leichte Panzerkompanie Ost (East Light Tank Company). By February 1941, this unit had only 10 TKS; the subsequent fate of these vehicles is unknown.

- **Romania**: in June 1937, the Poles sent a TKS and one of the two TKS-D to Romania for promotional purposes, but the Balkan country declined the offer.

- **Spain**: Republican Spain started negotiations to purchase 80 units, but the transaction did not take place because Poland maintained a policy of neutrality regarding the newly erupted civil war, which also earned it the support of the League of Nations. Unofficially, however, the Poles supplied the Republican front with weapons, spare parts, and some old Renault FT tanks, while they provided some old PSW-10 fighters to the Nationalist side.

- **Sweden**: in the 1930s, Sweden ordered a single TKS for testing and later requested between 20 and 60 units, but Poland did not respond positively.

- **Hungary**: on September 19, 1939, part of the 10th Mechanized Brigade found itself in Hungary after a painful retreat from invaded Poland. The Hungarian government interned the crews and seized 20 tankettes, including 4 TKS armed with 20 mm cannons. Subsequently, another 7 TKS and 9 TK-3 were incorporated into the Hungarian Army and used for auxiliary tasks.

- **Soviet Union**: on September 17, 1939, the USSR also attacked Poland and captured between 15 and 50 tankettes, to which were added the Estonian ones in the summer of 1940. The Polish vehicles were assembled into newly formed mechanized corps in the western territories for training purposes; some of these vehicles fought during Operation Barbarossa, particularly near Kiev.

SURVIVING UNITS

Only two TKS tankettes and one fully operational TK-3 have survived. All were reconstructed from wrecks in the first decade of the 21st century using non-original parts.

- 1 x TKS - One of the TKS tankettes was donated to Poland by the Swedish Tank Museum Axvall and has been on display at the Polish Army Museum since 2008. The Swedish TKS survived the post-war period in Norway, where it was used by a local farmer as a tractor.
- 1 x TKS - Private collection.
- 1 x TK-3 - Private collection.
- The other surviving tankettes are non-operational.
- 1 x TKS - On display at the Kubinka Tank Museum in Russia.
- 1 x TKF - Displayed at the Military Museum in Belgrade.
- 1 x TKS - Returned by the Norwegian Armed Forces Museum to the Armored Weapons Museum in Poznan, Poland.
- 1 x C2P artillery tractor - Found in Belgium and acquired by the National Military History Center in Auburn, Indiana, where it is currently on display.

▲ Beautiful picture with three Lutfwaffe skull soldiers in full battle gear leaning on a tankette.

TKS TANKETTE, POLAND 1939

TANKETTE TK/TKS

TWE | 45

▲ An abandoned TKS in Lipsko (Mazowieckie). The vehicle came from the Reconnaissance Tank Squadron of the Warsaw Armoured Brigade and was one of the most photographed wrecks of that September 1939.

▼ TKS placed in German service - probably immediately after the invasion of the USSR by the Nazis.

TKS TANKETTE, ESTONIA 1940

▲ TKS supplied by Poland to Estonia before the war.

TANKETTE TK/TKS

GERMAN PZKPFW TKS(P) USED IN FINLAND, SUMMER 1941

▲ PzKpfw TKS(p) reconnaissance tank of an unidentified Luftwaffe unit, Finland, summer 1941.

GERMAN PZKPFW TK(P) EAST FRONT, 1941

▲ PzKpfw TK(p) Panzer Company Warsaw, Governorate General 1941.

TANKETTE TK/TKS

GERMAN PZKPFW TKS(P) EASTERN FRONT 1941-1942

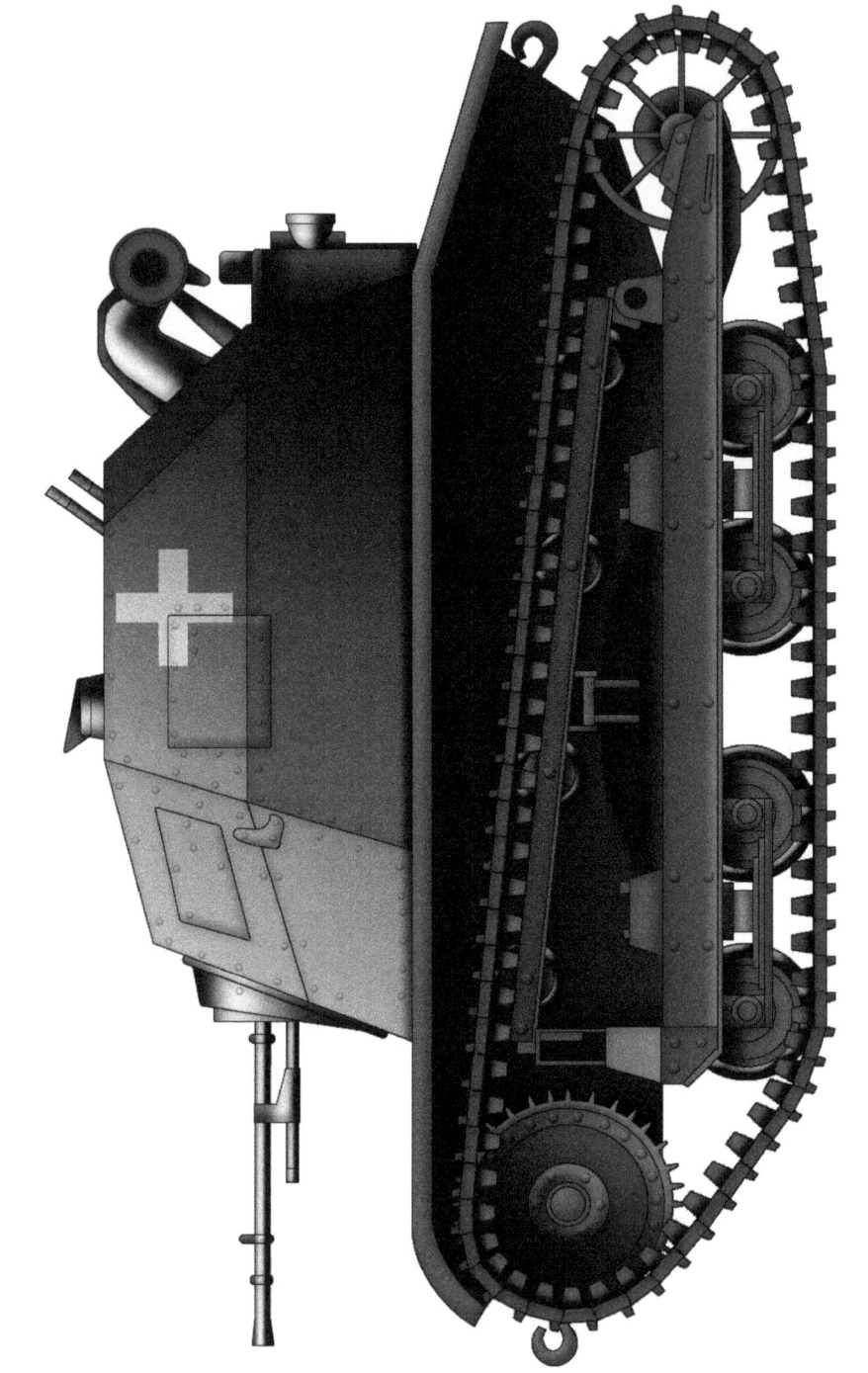

▲ PzKpfw TKS(p) reconnaissance tank of an unidentified unit, Eastern Front 1941-1942.

GERMAN PZKPFW TKS(P) IN NORWAY, 1942

▲ PzKpfw TKS(p) reconnaissance tank of an unidentified unit in Norway, 1942.

DATA SHEET				
	Carden-Loyd MK VI	TK-3	TKS	TKS 20 mm
Length	2,46m	2,58m	2,58m	2,58m
Width	1,7m	1,78m	1,79m	1,79m
Height	1,22m	1,32m	1,32m	1,32m
Weight in combat order	1400-1500 kg	2430 kg	2585 kg	2585 kg
Crew	2	2	2	2
Engine	32 CV	40 CV	45 CV	45 CV
Maximum speed	48 km/h	46 km/h	45 km/h	45 km/h
Autonomy	160 km	200 km	180 km	180 km
Tank capacity	38 l	70 l	70 l	70 l
Armour thickness	6-9 mm	3-8 mm	3-8 mm	3-8 mm
Armament	1-7,9mm Maxim wz.08	1 x 7.92 mm machine gun	1 x 7.92 mm machine gun	1-20 mm cannon

▲A highly unusual use of a TKS, here used to disguise a mock-up of a Soviet T-34 training tank. Bundesarchiv 5 November 1943.

GERMAN PZKPFW TKS(P) IN UKRAINE, 1943

▲ PzKpfw TKS(p) reconnaissance tank of an unidentified unit in Ukraine, 1943.

▲ The TKS tankette was a 'beutepanzer' par excellence. It fell into the hands of the Germans in good numbers in 1939 and was heavily reused by them..

▼ A tankette used by the Germans and later captured by the Allies is inspected by an American soldier in a Belgian warehouse used to collect material captured from the enemy.

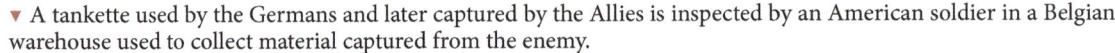

GERMAN PZKPFW TKS(p) EAST FRONT, 1943

▲ PzKpfw TKS(p) 'Schlepper' tractor of unidentified German unit, 1943.

SELF-PROPELLED TKD WITH 47MM CANNON, POLAND 1938

▲ TKD – 47 mm wz.25 Pocisk self-propelled infantry cannon, Poland 1938.

TKW WITH TURRET MOD. 1933, POLAND 1939

▲ A TKW made from an upgraded tankette with a 1933 model turret.

BIBLIOGRAPHY

- Ansell, David - *Ocskay Zoltán: Katonai motorkerékpárok*. Budapest, OldTimer média, 2007.
- Axworthy, Mark - Serbanescu, Horia: *L'esercito rumeno della seconda guerra mondiale*. Londra, Osprey Publishing Ltd., 1991.
- Barbarski, Krzysztof: *Armature polacche 1939-45*. Londra, Osprey Publications, Vanguard 30, 1982.
- Bonhardt Attila - Sárhidai Gyula - *Winkler László: A Magyar Királyi Honvédség fegyverzete*. Budapest, Zrínyi, 1992.
- Englert, Juliusz L. - Barbarski, *Krzysztof: Generale Maczek*. Londra, Istituto Sikorsky, 1992.
- Erdős László: *Katonai évkönyv 1936: Az összes államok haderejének ismertetése*. Budapest, Gergely R. Könyvkereskedése, 1936.
- David R. Higgins: *Panzer contro 7TP, Polonia 1939*. Oxford, Osprey Publishing, 2015.
- Jonac, Adam: *Tankietki TK-3 i TKS, WLU 18.*, Varsavia, Edipresse Polska, 2013.
- Jonac, Adam: *Pojazdy Mechaniczne Wojska Polskiego 1939*. Warsawa, ZP Grupa, 2010.
- Jonac. - Szubanski R. - Tarczynski J.: *Pojazdy Wojska Polskiego 1939*. Varsavia, WKL, 1990.
- Magnuski, Janusz: *Czolg Rozpoznawczy TK(TKS)*. Varsavia, MON, 1975.
- Majka, Jerzy: *Invincibile Brigata Nera: Polish 10th Cavalry Brigade 1939*. Sandomierz, Mashroom Model Publishing, 2010.
- McGilvray, Evan: *uomo d'acciaio e d'onore: Genereal Stanislaw Maczek*. Solihull, Helion Books, 2012.
- Nigel Thomas: *Hitler's Blitzkrieg Enemies 1940*, Oxford, Osprey Publication, 2014.
- Pielkalkiewicz, Janusz: *La cavalleria 1939-45*. Leicester, Macdonald, 1986.
- Pielkalkiewicz, Janusz: *Guerra dei carri armati 1939-1945*. Harborough, Guild Publishing, 1986.
- Porter, David: *Carri armati alleati occidentali 1939-1945*. Londra, Amber Books, 2009.
- Prenat, Jamie: *Polish Armor of the Blitzkrieg*, Oxford, Osprey Publications, New Vanguard 224, 2015.
- Tarnstrom, Roland: *La Polonia e le Repubbliche Baltiche*. H. n., 50 secoli di guerra, 1990.
- Surhone Lambert: *TKS: Tankette, Carden Loyd tankette, Invasion of Poland, Machine Gun, Panzer I, Panzer 35(t), Polish Army Museum, Kubinka Tank Museum*
- Szczerbicki, Tomasz: *Pojazdy Wojska Polskiego 1914-1939*. Czerwonak, Vesper, 2015.
- Zaloga, Steven: *Il carro armato leggero Renault FT*. Oxford, Osprey Publishing, 1988.
- Zaloga, Steven: *Blitzkrieg*. Londra, Arms and Armour, 1990.
- Zaloga, Steven - Madej, Victor: *The Polish Campaign 1939*, New York, Hippocrene Books, 1991.
- Zaloga, Steven: *Treni blindati*. Oxford, Osprey Publishing, 2008.

PUBLISHED TITLES

- ITALIAN LIGHT TANKS CV L3/33-35-38
- FOCKE-WULF FW 190
- SEMOVENTE 75/18 & 75/34
- ITALIAN MEDIUM TANK M13-40, M14-41 & M15-42
- PANZER III
- ITALIAN ARTILLERY 1914-1945 Vol.1
- PANZER II
- SOMUA S35
- FIAT C.R. 42 "FALCO"
- ITALIAN LIGHT TANK L6-40 & SEMOVENTE L40
- THE FIRST ITALIAN ARMOURED CARS: LANCIA 1Z, FIAT 611 AND OTHERS
- ITALIAN MEDIUM TANK M11-39
- HUNGARIAN TANKS TOLDI & TURAN
- PANZER 38 (t)
- ITALIAN ARTILLERY 1914-1945 Vol.2
- MATILDA MK II BRITISH TANK
- RUSSIAN LIGHT TANK T-26
- MESSERSCHMITT BF 109 Vol. 1 SERIE A-B-C-D-E
- M3 LEE/GRANT US MEDIUM TANK
- SEMOVENTI ITALIANI 2
- STUG III SD.KFZ. 142
- BLINDATI UNGHERESI ZRÍNYI E CSABA
- FIAT 3000 E FIAT 2000
- CANNONI ITALIANI 1914-1945 Vol.3

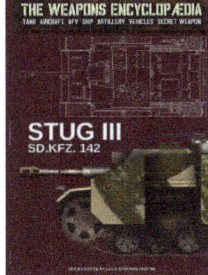

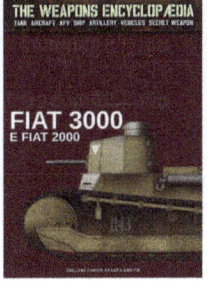

TWE-026 EN

www.ingramcontent.com/pod-product-compliance
Lightning Source LLC
LaVergne TN
LVHW072122060526
838201LV00068B/4951